A GUIDE FOR
YOUNG PITCHERS

A GUIDE FOR
YOUNG PITCHERS

Don Oster and Bill McMillan

THE LYONS PRESS
GUILFORD, CONNECTICUT
An imprint of The Globe Pequot Press

The Lyons Press is an imprint of The Globe Pequot Press.

10 9 8 7 6 5 4 3 2 1

Printed in the United States of America.

ISBN 1-59228-090-0

Library of Congress Cataloging-in-Publication Data is available on file.

ACKNOWLEDGMENTS

Bill and I would be remiss if we didn't acknowledge our sons who, as players, got us into the coaching business. Mike and Dave McMillan and Mark Oster had the toughest jobs on their teams while playing for their fathers. We must also recognize the contributions of the hundreds of young players we coached through the years. Included in this group are the coaches we worked with on different teams. Because of, or sometimes in spite of, our efforts, our teams managed to win most of their ball games. We learned many lessons from our players and in return trust that they learned from us. The most important reward was the fun we had.

We also need to recognize the patience and understanding of our wives, who supported us through many years of coaching. They didn't mind the time spent at games and practices and adjusted to continual late dinners during baseball seasons.

I personally owe a debt of gratitude to the efforts of a team that carried me to the Little League World Series in 1985. It was the experience of a lifetime, one never to be forgotten. Also, thanks to the hundreds of Little League pitchers I observed while umpiring. You can sometimes learn as much from watching someone do it wrong as you can when someone does it right.

Finally, thanks to members of the New Albany, Indiana, Township Little League organization, who assisted in the final phases of the book. Matt Kremer, Josh Santana, and Tony Kremer were a great help in the photo process.

Don Oster

CONTENTS

INTRODUCTION

Pitchers aren't born, they are developed. Pitchers come in all shapes and sizes and from all different kinds of backgrounds. You can pitch. Pitching is fun, and pitching and winning is more than double fun. Most young ballplayers want to try their hand at pitching but don't know how to start. This book will put you on the right track. With this guidance, you can learn how to be an effective pitcher.

First, there is one key question that only you can answer: Do you really want to pitch? The burning desire to be a pitcher must come from within. Be honest with yourself. Developing into a pitcher will take a lot of hard work, discipline, and dedication. The rewards for your work are obvious. If you don't want to pitch bad enough to pay the price, you'd be better off taking ground balls to develop into an infielder.

Over time, most pitchers, even those now pitching in the major leagues, have had to develop on their own. The following pages provide a course for you to follow to become a pitcher. You will learn about arm care, proper conditioning, and getting in shape to pitch. There are many keys to success, but very few pitchers can pitch consistently without using sound mechanics. Basic pitching mechanics are covered in both text and graphics.

How to practice and make it count toward your development is an important chapter. By applying the principles and instruction in the material, you can begin development on your own. You will learn the difference between throwing from the mound and pitching. Finally, the really fun parts to learn are the game strategies on how to pitch to the other team, work batters, and field your position.

Armed with all these tools, you will be well on the way to having the time of your life as a pitcher. And one last thing: Always remember to have fun.

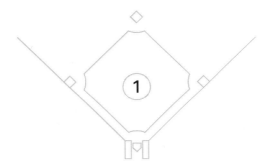

PROFILE OF A PITCHER

Coach has given the pitcher the ball. Little does the coach know that the pitcher would fight for the ball if necessary. This pitcher really wants to pitch more than anything else. The pitcher strides to the mound. This is not a cocky youngster, but the kid's body language says "I'm confident." The dirt around the rubber needs to be changed to feel comfortable. The pitcher uses a toe to carefully groom the area around the rubber.

This is where the player wants to be as either a starting pitcher or a reliever. No observer would doubt who is now in charge of the ball game. The pitcher may be a little nervous, but that is only normal. The facial expression is calm, and there is total focus on the task at hand. The pitcher knows every batter won't strike out, but the fielders will do their job. Each batter will first need to deal with good pitches to reach base. Free passes or walks will be few, if any. Batters will hit their way on base or else. This is a confident pitcher.

The warm-up pitches are crisp and in the strike zone. The windup is simple, smooth, and consistent. The pitcher's legs push off the rubber, helping the arm gain speed on the pitches. In a game, the pitcher can consistently throw strikes six or seven times out of ten pitches. In control drills without a batter, often times nine or ten out of ten pitches are strikes. Most of the pitches hit the catcher's mitt on the corners of the plate. This pitcher has good, sound pitching mechanics.

The pitcher's legs feel good. The arm is loose and strong. Pregame stretching and warm-up exercises have the body feeling ready for action. It has been hard work, but from the training program there is stamina to go the distance, if necessary. This is not the biggest, tallest, or strongest player on the team. None of this is necessary. The pitcher is in shape and is well-conditioned.

Throwing strikes is not a problem. Batters will need to work hard to get on base. The pitcher will know the game situation at all times, giving special attention to each batter's position in the other team's batting order.

The pitcher and catcher know how to work batters, read their stances, and pitch to their weaknesses. Mistakes made will provide opportunities to learn important lessons.

The pitcher may not have the best fastball in the league. It might be helpful but it is not necessary. There aren't a lot of batters this pitcher can blow away, but mixing pitch speeds will throw off a batter's timing. There is a plan and a purpose for each pitch. Self-control will be maintained no matter how tough the game situations become. The pitcher will always bear down, using many different approaches to get batters out. The difference between this pitcher and one who just goes to the mound and throws is that six inches between the ears. This is a smart pitcher.

To summarize, this is a smart, confident pitcher who has sound mechanics and is in good shape to pitch. This is a winning pitcher.

How do you get to this point? It starts with your desire to be a pitcher. Like we said before, you must want it enough to pay the price in terms of lots of hard work, discipline, and dedication. Everything else can be taught and developed, but the desire must come from you and only you.

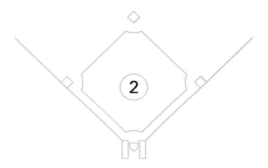

GETTING IN SHAPE TO PITCH

You use your whole body when you throw. If you want to be a good pitcher, it is important for you to get your whole body into good physical shape. Sports like hockey, skiing, basketball, soccer, and track help you get your body in shape and keep it that way. The every-day fun you have riding your bicycle, running, playing games, and doing exercises in gym classes also helps. Believe it or not, activities like ballet or karate that work on flexibility and balance are particularly good for pitchers. In short, stay active all year long. If you are in pretty good physical shape or have started a program to get into good physical shape, you can start getting into pitching shape.

CONCENTRATE ON FLEXIBILITY

Pitching uses muscles in a way that is different from almost any other sport. If you don't want to injure yourself, you must get those muscles in shape for pitching. The exercises and other pointers in this chapter are specially designed to teach your muscles to do the right things for proper pitching. Developing better flexibility is much more important for young pitchers than trying to develop strength. No special equipment or weights are necessary.

WHOLE BODY PITCHING EXERCISES

Jogging and Sprinting

Pitchers use their legs to generate power as they drive toward the plate. If you go to a major league game, you will always see pitchers jogging from foul line to foul line before the game. You will also see them running thirty- to fifty-yard sprints. You should get and keep your legs in shape because they are the foundation of your pitching power.

Jumping Jacks

Jumping jacks are a great exercise for fast body warm-up. You have probably done these hundreds of times. With jumping jacks you should concentrate on a smooth

rhythm from the starting position to the open position and back. Start with twenty repetitions at an even, smooth pace. Move up to forty when you feel ready. Do the first twenty very slowly, and do the next twenty at a fairly fast pace.

Crossover Toe Taps

Crossover toe taps are a warm-up exercise and a good stretching exercise for your back. You use your back a lot in pitching, so stretching it is important. For the fun

of it, and maybe better fielding, wear your glove when you do this exercise and do a backhand stretch when you reach to the opposite side.

Modified Hurdler Stretch

The modified hurdler stretch is designed to stretch the muscles in your leg and groin. Having flexibility in the leg and groin area is important, because the pitching action puts stress on this part of the body. Groin injuries sideline as many pitchers as arm injuries do (although usually not for as long).

In the hurdler stretch, you simply put your body in the position as shown in the illustration, first on one

side and then the other. You stretch until you can feel the strain in your upper legs and groin; then you hold it for a slow count of fifteen. Don't bounce. That could cause injury. If you keep working at this exercise, eventually you might be able to do a full split.

Arm Circles

Arm circles work on the specific muscles used in pitching. In this exercise you hold your arms straight out from your body and then slowly rotate them in narrow circles. The exercise is particularly good for your shoulder muscles and your upper back and chest muscles,

11

which are important in providing the power for pitching. Do twenty circles backward and twenty forward.

INDIVIDUAL ARM FLEXIBILITY EXERCISES

The next three exercises are designed to improve the flexibility of your pitching arm. You can do these exercises by yourself. They can be done when you are watching television or just sitting or standing. When you do these exercises, do not put too much pressure on your arm. When you feel the pressure, stop and hold the position.

Backward Hand Flex

This exercise stretches the muscles in the lower arm. You can feel the stretching just below your elbow on the inside of your arm.

Hold your pitching arm straight out in front of you. Reach over with the other hand and grab the fingers of your pitching hand. Pull them back slowly, with your arm straight, until you can feel the pressure just below your elbow. Hold it for a slow count of fifteen.

Fastball Arm Flex

When you throw a fastball, your arm rotates over the top of the ball after you release it, turning your palm outward. Start with your pitching arm straight out in front of you, palm down. Reach across with your other hand and grab the little finger side of your pitching

hand. Turn your pitching arm counterclockwise (if you are right-handed, clockwise if you are left-handed) so that your palm is away from your body until you feel the pressure in your elbow. Hold for a slow count of fifteen.

Reverse Arm Flex

This exercise is almost like the fastball arm flex, except that you rotate your arm in the other direction. Stretch your pitching arm out in front of you, palm up. Reach underneath with your other hand, and grab your pitching hand on the thumb side. Try to turn your arm clockwise (if you are right-handed, counterclockwise if you are left-handed), to bring the thumb toward the ground. When you feel pressure near your elbow, stop and hold it for a slow count of fifteen.

TWO-PERSON FLEXIBILITY EXERCISES

You will need another person to do the next four exercises. Exercising is usually more fun when you do it with someone else. Maybe you know someone who wants to pitch, and you can help each other. Pairing up with someone on your team at the start of practice is a convenient way to get these done. Be sure that your partner does not put too much pressure on your arm. When you feel the pressure say "stop."

Backward Extension

Put your arms straight behind you with your palms facing each other. Have your friend slowly bring your arms closer and closer together until you can feel the pressure in your shoulders. Then tell your partner to stop and hold it for a slow count of fifteen.

Now, with your arms still behind you, put the backs of your hands facing each other. Have your friend again slowly bring your arms closer and closer together. When you feel the pressure, tell your partner to stop and hold it for a slow count of fifteen.

Lay-back Flex

This exercise is designed to stretch the muscles in your shoulders and chest, which pull your arm forward when you throw. Hold your pitching arm straight out

sideways and bend your elbow. Have your helper support your elbow with one hand. Then with the other hand, your helper should slowly push your pitching arm backward until you can feel the pressure in the front of your shoulder. Hold this position for a slow count of fifteen.

Follow-Through Flex

Now, holding your elbow in the same position, rotate your arm until your fingers are pointing to the ground. Have your helper push the arm back until you can feel the pressure in your shoulder. Hold for a count of fifteen.

Full Rotation

The last exercise links the two exercises just described. Start in the lay-back flex and push all the way through

to the follow-through flex. Then move your arm back to the lay-back flex. Your helper should support your elbow and give you resistance both going forward and coming back. Repeat this exercise about twenty times. As you get stronger, have your helper give you a little more resistance.

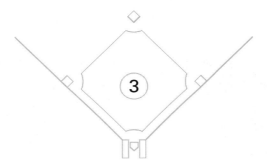

THE MECHANICS OF PITCHING

The movements a pitcher uses in pitching a baseball are called the mechanics of pitching. Pitchers have good mechanics when their movements are smooth, powerful, and coordinated.

Young pitchers with good mechanics:

- Have better control
- Put less strain on their arms
- Throw harder

Learning and practicing good pitching mechanics at an early age can make you a better pitcher now. Also, learning good mechanics now will save you a lot of problems later. Your arm will be healthy, and you will not have bad pitching habits to fix.

The picture sequence on the next two pages shows the entire pitching motion. This twelve-year-old pitcher has good mechanics as he goes through each important phase of the motion.

There are some key points about an effective pitching delivery that you can see in the picture sequence. Learn these key points and make yourself a better pitcher.

- Throw with a three-quarters arm motion. The three-quarters motion is halfway between throwing straight overhand (over the top) and sidearm. This motion is usually the most natural for young pitchers. Also, this motion will make the ball cross the strike zone at the hardest angle for batters to hit. Do not throw over the top. This motion puts too much strain on your shoulder and arm.

- Once you have developed good mechanics, try to throw each pitch exactly the same way. Using the same delivery every time will train your muscles to perform properly, and you will have better control. Also, you will not tip your change of speed pitches to the batter.

- Stay on balance throughout your delivery. Do not use a lot of wasted motion in your delivery because a herky-jerky delivery will upset your balance and cause you to lose control.

- Keep a "solid head." Keep your eyes on your target (the catcher's mitt) through the whole delivery. Some pitchers look up at the sky and others look at the ground or other places when they pitch. Taking your eyes off the target will only result in unnecessary adjustments during your delivery.

- Hide the ball from the batter. The less the batters see the ball the less chance they will have to adjust to your speed and location. They can't hit what they can't see. Hiding the ball from the batter starts at the beginning of the delivery and continues until it leaves your hand.
- Think "smooth and powerful." This thought will help you stay focused on using your body like a well-oiled machine.
- When you start your delivery, never stop for any reason. If you stop your delivery, the umpire will call a balk.

There are eight basic parts to the delivery. Doing each part well is necessary to have good mechanics. The pitcher in the pictures is right-handed. If you are left-handed, just substitute the word "left" with "right" here and throughout the book.

THE STANCE

The pitch begins with the stance. Stand comfortably on the rubber with the arches of your feet hanging over the front edge. Stand with both feet in the middle of the rubber. Now is the time to start hiding the ball. Use your glove to hide your grip from the batter. Your stance should be relaxed and your eyes should be focused on

the target. Some pitchers bend forward at the waist or put their pitching hand behind their backs. These additions to the basic stance add nothing to an effective delivery and are not necessary. Save the showmanship until you have your basic mechanics well under control.

THE STEP-BACK

From your stance, take a short, relaxed step backward with your left foot. Don't rush it. You are stepping back

so that you will have more power when you move toward the plate. Stepping back shifts most of your
weight to your left foot. As you step back, you should
raise your arms above your head. Bringing your arms
up will help you lay your pitching arm back more naturally when you get to that part of the delivery. If you
find that you lose your balance when you bring your
hands all the way over your head, you can try bringing
them just to your chest. Your left foot should be behind

the left side of the rubber so that you can move easily into the pivot.

THE PIVOT

Learning to use the pitching rubber properly will let you throw harder. The pitching rubber is not just a place to let pitchers know where to stand. It is one of the pitcher's best friends. A common mistake that young pitchers make is to try to pitch off of the top of the rubber. This will cause you to slip and lose your balance. You should push off from a firm place in front of the rubber. Pushing off the rubber gives you extra power in your legs. So, as you pivot your right foot, it should be placed sideways in front of the rubber like the pitcher in the picture. Your left shoulder and hip should be pointed toward the plate. There is no need to rush the pivot.

THE LEG LIFT (BALANCE POSITION)

When you move into the pivot, lift your leg as high as you can without losing your balance. Try to keep your left foot level with the ground like the pitcher in the picture. Try to keep your back straight. You should be in complete balance.

THE LAY-BACK

From the top of the leg lift position, your hands should come down and separate. You should stretch your pitching arm as far down and back as you can without losing balance. The farther you can lay your arm back, the harder you will be able to throw. Don't overdo this part. Many young pitchers can't fully extend their arms in this part of the delivery. As you get older, this full lay-back will be easier. Avoid "short-arming" the ball.

Young pitchers who bring the ball back only to their ear don't throw very hard.

THE STRIDE

You are now ready to drive toward the plate. You push off the rubber with your right foot and drive your left leg to a comfortable position with your left foot just to the left of a straight line toward home plate. Your left foot should land flat. You should not land on your heel. It is important to keep your left hip and shoulder pointed toward the plate. You will get more power this way. "Opening up" your hip and shoulder too soon will cause control problems. Having your hip and shoulder turned too far to the right will make you stride to the right. This is called "throwing across your body," and it is one of the major causes of arm injury.

THE RELEASE

In the end, where you release the ball will determine whether you throw balls or strikes. The place you release the ball is called "the release point." If your

pitches are too high, hold on to the ball a little longer. If they are too low, let go sooner. Many times you will get advice to lengthen or shorten your stride if you are pitching high or low during a game. If you have good mechanics, you took the stride you needed with you to the mound. During a game, you should correct the high and low balls with your release point. Finding the proper release point will not be difficult if you have sound mechanics. You will find that your release point may be slightly different from game to game. Good pitchers find their release point for all of their pitches when they warm up in the bull pen before they pitch.

When you look at a pitcher who has just released a fastball, you can see that the right hand and arm are turned very sharply to the right. There is no better example to show you why young pitchers should not throw curveballs. The curve is thrown by forcing your arm and elbow to turn in exactly the opposite direction from where they would naturally go. This is why throwing a curveball puts so much stress on a young pitcher's arm and elbow.

THE FOLLOW-THROUGH

After you release the ball, let your arm continue in the same motion. Let your arm follow through smoothly.

This smooth follow-through will allow the muscles in your arm and shoulder to relax naturally, which is an important purpose of the follow-through. You will hear people tell a pitcher who is throwing high to "follow through." You can see from the pitching sequence that when a pitcher follows through, the ball is already gone and the follow-through will not make the ball go any lower. The problem is with the release point, not the follow-through. If your mechanics are correct, you will finish your delivery directly facing the plate and ready to field your position.

WATCHING THE PROS

Understanding good mechanics will add to your enjoyment of watching professional pitchers. You'll notice that they do different things and pitch different ways. But you'll see that most of the pros have all the basic mechanics in their pitching motion. Once in a while you will see a pro who doesn't have good mechanics. You can expect to read about his sore arm troubles. The professional pitchers that many young pitchers like to copy are pitchers with strange deliveries. They pitch a little differently and are fun to imitate. It is fun but don't overdo it, and don't do it in a game. Major league pitchers who pitch in the majors for a long time are the ones who have good mechanics. So, have fun with pitching, but when you go to the mound, take your best mechanics with you.

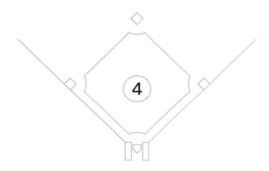

THE PITCHES

There are many types of pitches. All have some sort of name, but all of them have the same purpose—fooling batters. Fooling batters and striking them out is the pitcher's job. It's what makes pitching so much fun. Go to a pro game or watch a game on television and you'll see all kinds of pitches used. There are knuckleballs that flutter, curves, sliders, split-fingered sinkers, change-ups, and many more. But you will see more fastballs thrown than all other types combined.

In this chapter you will learn two pitches: a fastball and change-up. You can pitch effectively using these two pitches. At your age you are building a base for your future. It is in your best interest to concentrate more on developing sound pitching mechanics and good control than trying to mess with other pitches. As you mature and get stronger, you can start to experiment with other pitches, but your mainstay pitch will always be the good, controlled fastball that you develop now.

YOUR GRIP

Hold a ball in your pitching hand. If you have a small hand or shorter fingers, you may need to hold the ball back in your palm to get a secure grip on it. When your hand and finger size allows, you want to grip the ball with your fingers as far out from your palm as possible. The farther out on your fingers you can hold the ball

With-the-seams two-fingered grip

Across-the-seams two-fingered grip

and control it, the harder you will be able to throw and get movement on your fastball.

There are two basic grips, as you can see in the photos. Using the with-the-seams two-fingered grip, your index and middle fingers are along and in contact with the seams at their narrowest point. With the against-the-seams grip, your fingers are across the seams, again

With-the-seams three-fingered grip

Across-the-seams three-fingered grip

at their narrowest point. The thumb also contacts a seam when using both grips. If your fingers and hand are too small to get a good grip on the ball with either of the two-fingered grips, use three fingers either with or across the seams. Experiment with the different grips and find the one that is most comfortable. Then stick with it as long as it works for you.

THE FASTBALL

The fastball has been given many names. It is called the "heater," "smoker," "blazer," "hummer," "burner," and many others. Pitchers with extremely hard fastballs may be called "flamethrowers" or "a guy who can really bring it." Batters may say a pitcher is so fast it looks like he's throwing aspirin pills. Major league scouts scour the country looking for pitchers with a blazing fastball. They believe they can teach a pitcher control, but they can't teach a good heater. It requires time and work to develop a good fastball.

Don't be discouraged if your fastball doesn't have "the pop" in the early stages of your career. You haven't reached maturity yet. Develop good sound mechanics, stay in shape, and keep developing control of your fastball. Learn to throw your fastball with exactly the same motion and delivery every time. Strength and pitch speed will come naturally as you grow and continue to develop.

OK, you've selected a grip that is most comfortable. Now, hold the ball as far out in your fingers as your hand will allow and make your pitches. As you release the fastball, slightly snap your wrist forward. This slight movement will cause the fingers to bend backward, pulling down on the ball as it starts toward the plate. As your pitch speed increases, there is a point where your fastball will tail, move, or slide. This "live" fastball is much harder for batters to hit.

Some left-handed pitchers are blessed with not being able to throw a straight pitch. For some reason, their fastball "tails" as soon as they throw it fast enough that it doesn't go in a rainbow arc toward the plate. To their advantage they will usually have a natural live fastball.

THE CHANGE-UP

Even at the major league level there are many pitchers who succeed using only fastballs mixed with change-ups. The slower speed in a good change-up is the main thing that fools the batters and disrupts their timing. There may also be some movement on a change-up caused by different grips. We won't bother with trying to get movement on your change-up now. The speed difference alone will serve you just fine. You can work on a change-up that moves or slides in a few years when you've matured. For now you'll work on mastering the straight change-up. It is the second of your two main tools.

So far we haven't really talked about pitch speed. Given your age, physical development, and mechanics, your fastball is at some level of speed. A change-up is a pitch that simply is not quite as fast as your normal fastball. It should be about 80 to 85 percent as fast as your fastball. You want it to be slower and look like your fastball but still have enough speed that the batter can't recover and hit it.

There are two basic ways for a young pitcher to throw a change-up. First, using exactly the same windup and motion, throw the ball, but just not as hard as you would your fastball. Another way to throw a change-up is, again using the same motion, to bury the ball way back in the palm of your hand and use a three or four-fingered grip. If getting the ball out on the fingers increases pitch speed, burying it in the palm makes it almost impossible to throw hard. This difference in speed is enough to fool most batters. Experiment with both methods to see which one you can control the best.

Why throw a change-up? One of the pitcher's most effective weapons is the ability to mess with a batter's timing, and this is the main purpose of the change-up. Batters can time your fastball after they've seen it a few times. If you stay with constant speed pitches, good hitters will soon figure you out. Develop a good change-up that you can control, and you will be able to keep most of the batters off balance.

OTHER PITCHES

When other people learn that you are a pitcher, some of them will want to show you how to throw a pitch.

Chances are it will be some kind of slider or a curveball. These people mean well and think they are helping you, but they're not. Thank them, then file their advice away until later. The pitch someone suggests may be a very good one that you'll learn to use later in your career. But don't be tempted to try throwing it now.

You may have goofed around trying to throw a curveball, slider, or other breaking pitch. It could be fun to make a batter whiff at a breaking pitch, but in the long run all you will get is a sore arm. The wrist and arm snap required to spin the ball, which makes a pitch break or curve, requires a stress that has ruined countless young arms well before they ever had a chance to grow and develop. The time for developing breaking pitches will come soon enough when you are in your mid-teens.

Pick up the sports page and on many days you will read about a top pitcher going on the disabled list with a sore arm. Worse yet, some press releases announce that a certain pitcher is having arm or shoulder surgery. In most cases, these arm injuries are the direct result of throwing curveballs and sliders. Leave these pitches alone for now. After all, you're too young to go on the disabled list!

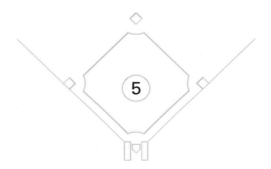

PRACTICING PITCHING

Pitchers need to practice a lot. Good pitchers will practice even more. The best way to get the practice you need is in an organized youth league. If you are fortunate enough to be on a team with good coaches or pitching coaches, they will work specifically with the pitchers. They will have pitchers throw on a regular schedule, gradually increasing the workouts until the team is ready for the season. In the northern climates, the early workouts are usually held indoors. A pitcher should have at least four weeks of structured practice to be ready to pitch in games.

If you are not in a program or on a team, or your coach doesn't have time to practice with you, this chapter will tell you how to train and practice pitching on your own.

PRACTICE OBJECTIVES

These are your practice objectives:

- *Conditioning*—Get your arm, legs, and body in shape to pitch.
- *Mechanics*—Develop the strong, smooth mechanics that are needed for consistent, good pitching.
- *Pitches*—Work on developing your fastball and change-up.
- *Control*—Work on pitch control, throwing strikes at first, then spotting your pitches.
- *Confidence*—Build confidence that you can throw a strike at any time.

FIND A CATCHER

Up to a point, anyone who can squat down and catch the ball can work out with you. It is best if you can find a player who enjoys catching and wants to become a good catcher. Make sure the catcher has all of the protective equipment. You don't want anyone getting hurt. If you worry about throwing a bad pitch that could hurt your catcher, you won't throw your best.

Finding a catcher isn't easy. Catching is the toughest job on a baseball team and most players want no part of it. It is great if you can work with your team's catcher. The teamwork needed to work on batters can be developed during your practice sessions. If you can't find a catcher, an option is to find another player who wants to pitch, borrow some equipment, and trade off catching duties.

FIND A PLACE TO WORK OUT

The field where you play games is absolutely the best place to practice. A softball field is okay, too, but if no fields are available, a level place in a park or backyard will do. There must be enough room to throw. The regulation Little League distance from the front of the pitcher's plate or rubber to the back of home plate is forty-six feet, six inches. Allowing room for the catcher, a sixty-foot-long distance will be fine for practice. You need a backstop of some kind. Nothing makes practice more of a pain than having to stop to retrieve the ball. If you don't have a mound to throw from, don't worry. The regulation Little League mound is only six or eight inches high.

If the outdoor place where you will practice doesn't have a rubber or pitcher's plate, you need to make one. You will push off from it when you make your pitches. To make a rubber, cut a length of board two feet long, four or five inches wide, and a one-half-inch thick. Drive two or three heavy nails through the board. The nails will anchor your portable rubber to the ground. Also make a home plate by cutting a seventeen-inch long by ten-inch wide strip from a piece of carpet, cardboard, or wood.

If the weather is too bad to practice outdoors, look for a place indoors. In Minnesota, for example, pitchers practice in school gyms, barns, or big garages. You will need to use one of the stripes on a gym floor or put tape on a garage floor for a rubber. Neither of these is any good to use as a push-off point, but it's better than not practicing at all. Go to a store, buy a couple of good regulation leather baseballs, oil up your glove, round up your catcher, and you're ready for practice.

STARTING OUT RIGHT

Always warm up before picking up the ball to throw. Jog and do some stretches and side-bends until you feel loose. Also, do the finger, wrist, arm, and shoulder flex exercises you learned in Chapter 2. Put your catcher through the flex exercises. You don't want your partner to have arm problems either.

After making soft tosses for about ten minutes, or until your arm feels good and loose, begin pitching.

Fifteen is about the average number of pitches in an inning. To work an inning set, make fifteen pitches, then rest. Throw no harder than medium speed at first. Concentrate on making a smooth, consistent delivery. Have your catcher hold a target down the middle. Without aiming, try to make each pitch a strike. Ask the catcher to count the strikes in each set.

MAKE SOME MARKERS

During your first set, make a couple of markers. First draw a straight line from the middle of the rubber directly toward home plate. Go through your full delivery and hold your follow-through position. If the pitch was good and felt right, look down at your lead foot. If it is on or nearly on the direct line toward the plate, this is where you want it to be every time.

Next note the length of your stride and mark it, too. Hitting the line toward the plate and having a consistent stride length are two basic elements of sound mechanics and control. Remember these markers and refer to them occasionally. They will be valuable tools to help you solve control problems.

Try to practice every two or three days. During the first week, work only two fifteen-pitch sets—again not throwing hard. During breaks between sets and after

PITCHER'S PLATE

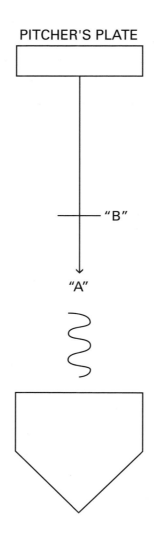

"B"

"A"

MARKERS

Starting from the point where you plant your foot, make a line "A" from the pitcher's plate toward home plate. This is your directional marker. Following several good pitches, put a "B" where your lead foot lands. This is your normal stride length.

each workout, put your arm in a jacket sleeve. You should let your arm cool gradually after throwing. After four or five workouts, add a third set. After another four or five workouts, add a fourth set.

LISTEN TO YOUR BODY

As you increase the inning sets, pay particular attention to how you feel. At the first sign of feeling tired in either your arm or legs, put on your jacket and stop practice. You won't have a good workout if you're tired, and you may risk having a sore arm. When you have worked up to five sets, start throwing hard in the last two sets.

It is hard to say how soon you will get to your maximum full workouts of throwing hard for six full sets. You won't need to go any further in terms of numbers of sets, but you should reach this level in about four or five weeks of practice. Pay close attention to your strike counts as you begin to throw harder. Don't abandon your good, smooth delivery as you increase your speed. If you begin to lunge or rush your delivery, your control will suffer. Keep your delivery smooth and powerful.

THROW STRIKES, WORK LOW

Your catcher is counting strikes in each set. As soon as you can throw an average of ten strikes in every fifteen-pitch set, have the catcher start moving the target to different parts of the strike zone. Imagine that the strike zone is a window in front of the catcher. It has four panes; two above and two below. The top of the window is at a batter's letters; the bottom is at his knees. Have the catcher move the target back and forth in the bottom two panes of your window. This will have you throwing low in the strike zone. Low fastballs and change-ups will always be your money pitches. You will learn more about them in later chapters.

READY?

After you have worked out for about four weeks, you should be confident that you can throw a good hard strike at any time. Keep your change-up low and its speed at about 80 percent of your fastball. Your mechanics should be sound and your muscle memory conditioned to keep your delivery consistent. You should also be able to go for six full sets without tiring. In the next chapter we'll add a batter to fine-tune your control, and the pitching window will take on more meaning.

In your youth league program, you should be ready to pitch about the time serious practices start. If your coaches haven't seen you pitch before, find a way to let them know that you are a pitcher. When they give you a look, you will be able to show them that you are ready.

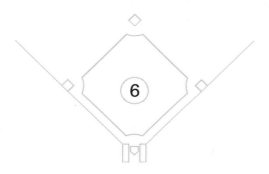

CONTROL

PITCH CONTROL

You can and will throw strikes consistently. Throughout
your practice sessions your catcher has counted strikes.
In a fifteen-pitch set you should strive to throw at least
ten strikes, sometimes a few more. Attaining this level is
very good, especially as you begin to throw harder.

Learn to Spot Pitches

Now we'll put icing on the cake. You're in good condition and can go six sets without tiring. Your mechanics
are sound and your motion is smooth. Your strike
count is good, even when you throw hard and mix in

change-ups. In this later stage of your practices for the season, you need to find another volunteer—a batter. Have anyone of normal height, wearing a batting helmet, stand in the batter's box while you work some of your sets.

Consider the strike zone to be from the batter's knees to the upper chest. Ask your catcher to hold targets in different parts of the strike zone. Work to the batter low and inside, then low and away. Make sure the catcher keeps the target low most of the time. Strikes are good, low strikes are even better. Don't be timid about pitching inside. Nibble at the inside corner of the plate with the same concentration as the outside corner and mix in a change-up once in a while. Also have the catcher hold a high target at the batter's shoulder level. You will sometimes use this unhittable pitch to fool a batter when you're way ahead in the count.

Work to a Lefty

Even if most batters are right-handed, don't ignore the other side of the plate. Some pitchers are so unfamiliar with pitching to a left-handed batter, that they almost give them a free pass to first. Have your batter spend enough time in the left-hand batter's box for you to become familiar with pitching to a lefty. Even if the batter is left-handed, the strike zone doesn't change.

Work Longer

Pick a set in the middle of your workouts and try throwing a longer distance. Back away to a distance of about fifty-five feet (three long steps behind the rubber), and pitch a set. After a rest, move back to the standard forty-six-foot rubber to pitch the next set. If you have thrown strikes from the longer distance, it should seem easier from the shorter distance. If this helps, you may use a few longer pitches in a pregame warm-up.

Solving Control Problems

If you start having problems throwing strikes, the first thing to do is check your markers. Is your plant foot landing on or near the line toward the plate? Missing the line can cause pitches to be off the plate either to the inside or outside. You want to be near the line on each pitch. Check to see if your stride length is consistent. Lengthening or shortening your stride from pitch to pitch can cause a high or low control problem.

Does your control change when you throw harder? You must resist any tendency to lunge or get off balance when you try to rev it up a notch. Some pitchers have a tendency at times to rush their delivery without realizing they have changed. Continue to check your markers and concentrate on a smooth powerful delivery. Keep the same motion, throwing your change-up for strikes. If there are problems, check the same things you would check for the fastball.

Never Aim

Spotting pitches will be a big part of your success in getting batters out consistently. Don't expect to hit the target on each pitch. Stay with your consistent mechanics and do not aim your pitches. Changing your normal delivery and aiming the ball will only get you in trouble. Usually when a pitcher tries to aim, control gets worse.

SELF-CONTROL

Throughout the course of a game, you may experience a wide range of emotions. How well you control these emotions can be a major factor in how well you pitch. When you go to the mound, you should be excited, keyed up, and ready to pitch your best. It is also normal to be a little nervous, because it shows that you care a lot about the outcome of the game. To be a good pitcher, you need to keep your cool and channel your nervous energy into focusing on the job of getting batters out.

When everything is going well, keeping good self-control is easy. Pitching is a ton of fun when the batters are whiffing at your pitches and the fielders are making highlight plays on the few balls that are hit. Life is good when your control is sharp, you're nibbling at the corners, and batters are screwing themselves into the ground after missing swings at your change-up.

Keep Your Cool

Many potentially good pitchers have failed because they couldn't control their emotions. It is certain that trouble will come in a ball game. The real test of your self-control is how you behave when everything goes wrong. Say you are working hard and doing your best in a game, but your control is a little bit off. Your infielders boot two ground balls in a row, playing worse than six-year-old T-ballers. To make matters worse, the umpire has been struck with temporary blindness, calling four balls in a row on reasonably good pitches.

You should be finished with the inning, but now you're standing on the mound with no outs and the bases loaded. The other team has on its rally caps, fans are screeching, and your coach is having fits in the dugout. If you can keep your cool in a situation like this, you have the makings of a good pitcher. If you can keep your cool and actually want to take on this challenge, you may have the makings of a very good relief pitcher. More on this later.

Dealing with Stress

Stress or tension is your worst enemy. It can cause you to doubt your ability, think negative thoughts, and actually make your muscles tighten. To deal with stress in a situation like this you need time to calm down. First, take a deep breath to relax. You may also walk behind the mound, play with the rosin bag, or call your catcher out for a conference. You want to feel the tension leaving your body. Remember, this is only a game; they don't shoot the losing pitcher.

It may be easy to blame everyone else for the fix you're in, but that won't help. You can't think about what has happened. There aren't any do-overs in baseball, and no miracle will make the runners disappear. This jam is yours to deal with. You can only gather yourself together and focus on the next batter and the next one after that and the next . . . It may be time to strike one out, or the defense may get a double play. Do your best. Your teammates may get a lot of runs and things may work out after all. But if it doesn't, stay confident; you'll get them next time.

Don't set yourself up for disappointment. You must have confidence in yourself. But know that there will be days, just like there are for even the best pitchers, when you get hit hard. At times your pitch control won't be the best or your defense will go on vacation. You won't win every game. Sometimes you will pitch really well and your team won't score enough runs. Don't worry about these things. Keep your cool, do your best, and things will work out.

Relief Pitchers

Good relievers must have excellent pitch and self-control. The starter sees trouble develop gradually in the game. The reliever usually inherits a mess from the start, and many times the game is on the line. A reliever cannot afford to let stress or emotions get in the way of doing the job. No matter how bad the situation, relievers must calmly focus on going after the first batter they face. Some relievers actually thrive on chaotic situations and welcome any chance to pitch under pressure.

SUMMARY

Pitch Control

- Spot pitches, and work low and over the corners.
- Practice pitching to a lefty.
- Keep smooth, powerful mechanics.
- Check your markers to help fix control problems.
- Don't aim the pitches or rush your delivery.

Self-Control

- Keep your cool and stay confident.
- Keep a positive attitude.
- Deal with tension and stress.
- Expect to be good but not perfect every time.

PREPARING TO PITCH A GAME

Your games don't happen on the spur of the moment. They are scheduled and you know, barring weather problems, when you're going to play. On the day you are going to pitch, take it as easy as you can. It is a good idea to stay out of the swimming pool and not do a lot of strenuous exercise. It is usually hot during your season. You'll need all of your energy for the game. If it's really hot on game day, try to spend most of the day in a cool place. Consider taking a small cooler of ice and a couple of old towels to the game. Putting iced towels on your neck or head can help you cool down between innings. Also drink plenty of cool water.

In this chapter you will learn about game preparation before throwing the first pitch.

THE STARTER

Being a winning pitcher starts well before the first pitch. First, you must loosen up by jogging and doing both body and arm stretching exercises. This is the same warm-up routine you followed during preseason practice. On a warm day, start your warm-up pitches early enough to throw for ten to fifteen minutes and rest for about five minutes before going to the mound. If the weather is cool, extend your warm-up pitches to up to twenty minutes.

Start the warm-up with easy throws, then throwing harder as you loosen up. Work on your control and get the feel of a nice, smooth delivery. Throw only as long as it takes to throw your hardest. Don't use yourself up in the bull pen; save your best for the game. As soon as you can throw your hardest with good control, put a jacket on your arm to keep it warm and go to the dugout. You're ready.

THE RELIEVER

In pro ball, relief pitchers loll around in the bull pen until a call comes from the dugout to "get someone up." The relief pitcher usually has time to warm up before entering the game. This is seldom the way it happens in Little League games. Although there may be as many as four pitchers on a roster, most of the pitchers also play a defensive position when they aren't pitching. Seldom will coaches sit a good player who is also a pitcher just to have a relief pitcher when they need one.

Let's say you are playing shortstop in the fifth inning and trouble arises. The starter has tired and walked a couple of batters. There is one out when the coach goes to the mound, calls you over, and gives you the ball. Unless the other pitcher is being replaced because of an injury, you will only get about eight warm-up pitches before facing the next batter. Without a sufficient warm-up, you can hardly expect to do your best. If you aren't prepared, this situation can also lead to a sore arm.

You should find out from the coach before the game if you are scheduled to relieve. As a reliever, you may have a tough time staying ready to take the mound. You may be loose from pregame warm-ups at the start of the game, but you will need to do more during the course of the game to be able to go in and be effective at any time. When you're not batting, throw easy on the sideline with another player during the third or fourth inning. If a catcher is available, go through a quick pregame warm-up. Place your arm in a jacket sleeve to keep it from cooling between innings. It is best if you are allowed to start an inning, giving you time to really warm up on the sideline. However, relievers don't get to pick the time when they enter the game.

THE MOUND

The mound is your territory. Before taking any warm-up pitches, make sure it is groomed the way you want. You must have a firm footing to pitch from. Any loose dirt or holes can affect your delivery and control. Check the rubber. The top should be even with the dirt, and there should be a solid flat place in front of it where you can place your foot when you push off during your delivery. Some pitchers leave a hole in front of the rubber. Either use the hole or fill it in. Make the rubber comfortable for your use.

Look at the spot where your lead foot will land. You want a firm place so your foot won't slip or slide as you complete your delivery. Brush any loose dirt away from your landing spot. Check and fix these areas before starting to warm up for each inning. Call time out, if necessary, to fix the mound during any inning.

SCOUT THE OTHER TEAMS

To be a good pitcher you need to study batters. The best way is to watch games in your league. You will be looking for batter weaknesses. After watching a team bat a couple of times, you should know who the best hitters are and what pitches they prefer. Watch for batters who want to bunt their way on base. You'll see which batters are suckered by high pitches and seldom make contact. Make note of slow swingers, loopy swingers, pull hitters, and lookers who are begging for a walk. You'll learn how to pitch to each of these and more in the next chapter. The important thing for now is that you know some of their weaknesses.

THE SCORE BOOK

Someone on your team keeps a score book. The book can give you valuable information on the other team's batters. Take a quick look at the score book notations for the last time you played the team. Discuss known strengths and weaknesses of the batters with your catcher. For the best hitters, suggest where you want the target and how you want help working these batters. Each bit of information you can gather plus teamwork gives you an edge to help get batters out.

THE PITCH COUNT

Depending on your size, strength, and physical condition, you will have somewhere between seventy and ninety pitches in your body for a game. This is why conditioning and throwing strikes are so important. It varies by individual, but most pitchers in the ten- to twelve-year-old age group start to hit a wall of fatigue at around seventy to seventy-five pitches. As the pitch count nears one hundred, most young pitchers become too tired to be effective. Your coach should have the scorer keep the pitch count and be aware of how many pitches you should throw.

As your pitch count reaches the sixties, the coaches should be looking for early signs of tiring. Tell your coaches if you're beginning to tire. They should have a reliever ready to take your place. Although it may seem heroic to stick it out, the award for overuse of your arm at your age can be soreness that doesn't benefit anyone. You will live to pitch another day.

AFTER THE GAME

Most league rules set a maximum number of innings a pitcher can pitch in a week. There are also usually rules for days of rest for pitchers between games. These are good rules, intended to protect young arms. How well you use days off can let you rest your arm and set you up for a good performance the next time out.

Preparation to pitch the next game begins immediately following a game you've pitched. As soon as possible, ice your arm. Don't ice it so long as to get frostbite, but you should immerse it in ice water or put ice packs around your elbow and forearm until they are very cool. The ice will help relieve any minor swelling and soreness.

With any luck you can rest your arm the day following a strenuous game. If your team has a practice the next day, go easy on your arm. At the next practice (after a prepractice warm-up of arm and body exercises), pair off with a teammate. Start with some easy tosses at a close range of about thirty feet. As you start to feel loose, gradually back up until you are at a "long toss" distance of about sixty feet apart. Don't throw hard. Go through a fully extended motion, throwing just hard enough to lob the ball to your partner in a nice medium-high arc. Five to ten minutes of long toss should help relieve any stiffness in your arm from the previous game.

When you are in infield or outfield practice, take care not to make hard throws for at least two days following the game you pitched. Warm up, do the long toss, and rest your arm as much as possible. On the third day following a game, if your arm feels good, you may do two or three medium-speed control drill sets with your catcher. Having rested and lightly worked out for three days, you should be ready to resume a full workout on the fourth day.

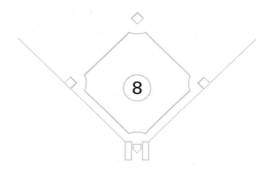

PITCHING TO BATTERS

There is good reason why the pitcher and catcher are called the "battery." You two are the part of the team that gets it started and keeps it running. Your catcher should be your best friend on the team. Together, your teamwork and how well you work the batters will make a big contribution to a winning season. Understanding how to pitch to different batters is where your catcher can support you best. The catcher might see things about batters that you don't. The better your catcher understands pitching, the better you can work together as a team.

PACE

We've already talked about your control of the pace of the game (with the possible limitation of enforcement of the twenty-second rule, which requires that the pitcher deliver a pitch within twenty seconds of receiving the ball, when there are no base runners). Here's how it can work in your favor. When batters take their stance in the batter's box, most of them are a little tense. The longer they stand there, the more their muscles tighten. So take a few seconds between pitches. As you relieve any tension you feel, the batter's tension increases. A batter's muscle tension works to your advantage. Most batters can't swing normally when their muscles are tight. In fact, some batters may get so nervous that they'll swing at anything you throw. There are a couple of batter types you can successfully use this tactic on.

Now we'll look at several different batters and talk about how to pitch to them. As you pitch to these batters, we will suggest pitch locations where they have difficulty hitting effectively. You should try to pitch to those locations as often as you can. However, there will be times when your control is not exactly great. When that happens, just throw strikes. Make them hit the ball and trust your defense. Nothing is worse than trying to nibble around the corners and end up walking batters. They'll just send another one to the plate.

GET AHEAD

With that in mind, remember that one of your most effective weapons is a first-pitch strike. A strike on the first pitch does two good things: First, the strike gets you ahead in the count and puts a little more pressure on the batter. Second, it challenges the batter and lets you serve notice that there are no free tickets to first base today. Most batters are not good first-pitch hitters; they want to see a pitch to try to time your fastball.

If you're making the first pitch too good, some teams may catch on and start ripping it. Then it's time to pitch more carefully and mix them up. Try to bait them outside with the first pitch. Maybe a first pitch high at the shoulders will bring a big whiff. If they are intending to go for the first pitch, they may swing at anything.

LOOKERS

You might also call these batter types "beggars." They come to the plate begging for a walk. Perhaps the coach has told some batters to "just get on base," and they figure that if they stand in the box, you'll walk them. You'll likely find a looker or two in the lower part of the batting order. They may look sort of timid when they come to the plate and may crouch down in their stance to make the strike zone smaller. But the easiest way to identify lookers is that they seldom swing at a pitch. You pop your first strike right down the middle and the bat doesn't move on either that pitch or the next one. If a looker does swing, it is usually a hesitant, halfhearted effort. Give this batter your best fastball strikes. Send the lookers back to the dugout and remember them when they come to bat again.

PLATE CROWDERS

The crowder steps into the batter's box and sets up right on the edge of the plate. The hands may even be over the inside corner. A plate crowder is trying to take the plate away from you. Many pitchers are so afraid of hitting a batter that they will not pitch inside. If so, crowding the plate will draw a lot of walks. Or, maybe the batter who hangs ten over the edge of the plate wants an outside pitch to hit.

None of this matters. Remember that the plate is yours. As a pitcher, you are entitled to try to pitch over any part of it. There is no suggestion here that you throw at a batter. You are not throwing at batters when you pitch inside no matter where they take their stance. Pitch the plate crowder inside, low and inside if possible. Any inside pitch that the crowder contacts

will usually be a weak handle hit. If you let a batter take half of the plate away and this ends up with that batter walking to first base, the fault is yours. If you miss on a pitch and throw it too far inside, the batter must get out of the way. A pitch that hits the batter's body when it is in the strike zone is a strike. After all, plate crowders are asking for close pitches when they crowd the plate.

LATE SWINGERS

The bat may be too heavy, or the batter can't quickly decide to swing, or your fastball is too quick. None of this matters; the late swinger's bat goes through the strike zone after your fastball has passed. Look for this batter type in the lower part of the batting order. You and your catcher should be able to easily spot this one. The ball may even be in the catcher's mitt when the

batter swings. Don't get cute and try to play with a late hitter, and never throw a change-up to a late swinger or just plain bad hitter. Change-up speed is the only pitch slow enough for the late swinger to hit. Give this batter a steady diet of fastballs. A foul tip may be the best effort for a late swinger.

PULL HITTERS

These batters make a big stride down the line with their lead foot as the pitch arrives. Bona fide pull hitters will be looking for a pitch down the middle or a little inside. They want the pitch around or slightly above the waist. They look for a pitch they can turn on and drive out of the yard. A pull hitter may have had the misfortune of hitting a home run early in the season and has decided to go for the title.

The pull hitter will usually swing really hard and get way off balance on the follow-through. With this batter, it's all or nothing. So give a pull hitter nothing inside, unless it's very low or chin high. The best pitch to this batter type is low and away. Few batters have the strength to pull an outside pitch. Even fewer pull hitters know how to go with an outside pitch and hit it to the opposite field. Outside pitches to pull hitters usually result in a ground ball to either the second-baseman or shortstop.

SCARED BATTERS

A scared batter may have been a plate crowder until he or she got plunked by a fastball. This batter will set up with either an extreme open stance (front foot down the line), or be square in the box but so far away from the plate that the bat arc doesn't come close to the outside half of the plate. Scared batters will be clearly set

up far away from where the pitches will pass. Pitch this one on the outside corner.

ANXIOUS BATTERS

Anxious batters have happy feet in the batter's box. They dance around like they have ants in their pants. They make quick little half-swings with the bat as if they're trying to work up to something. Some anxious batters are very good hitters. All the mannerisms and movement may be a way of staying loose. However, if they're so anxious to get at you, let each one wait a bit. Use your legal time looking in toward the catcher as if you are getting a sign. If the anxious batter is really ready, throw a fastball way outside or up near the ears. The anxious one might chase it. If the batter looks to be swinging ahead of the pitch, throw a change-up. Keep the next fastball down and in or down and away, and you will probably send this batter dancing back to the dugout.

BIG LOOPY SWINGERS

Watch a batter's warm-up swings to spot a loopy swinger. The arms on these batters are almost fully extended when the bat goes through the strike zone. The bat may seem to be swinging the batter. This batter may also be a late swinger. Throw hard, inside fastballs and also work low and away on the outside corner. It's doubtful that a loopy swinger can hit anything but a down-the-middle perfect pitch. If, in the unlikely event that this batter gets you timed, a low inside change-up should be the ticket.

NERVOUS BATTERS

White knuckles from choking the bat too tight, a taut stance, clenched teeth, and a worried expression distinguish nervous batters. This is another type you'll find near the bottom of the batting order. If batters are nervous when they step into the batter's box, make their tension work for you. Again, find a way that is not obvious to take your time between pitches. Let the batters stand there, getting more tense and tied up as they wait for each pitch. The tension that builds up as these batters wait only makes them less harmful to your cause. Some may tighten up to the point that they can barely make a swing. Give nervous batters the slow treatment and then three fastball strikes.

GOOD HITTERS

You'll find the good hitters in the top four or five positions in the order. They look confident when they stride to the plate and dig in. They usually have quick wrists and a tight compact swing. The stance is usually straight and they stride toward the pitcher when they swing. Good hitters either can hit for power or go with the pitch to either field. Don't be afraid of this batter, although you will need to pitch carefully. The good hitter's

batting average probably isn't much above .400. You have a 60 percent chance of getting an out.

Many good hitters are proud, too proud to take a walk. Good hitters are also aggressive, having gotten the notion that they can hit any pitch hard. These two factors may enable you to work low and inside and low and away, getting a pop-up or ground-out on a bad pitch. Try not to get behind on the count—you want the batter to hit your pitch. Try to throw your fastball past a good hitter. As soon as the batter gets your fastball timed, throw a low change-up. Mix speeds and locations, low inside and low outside. Remember, teams put good hitters out six times out of ten.

BUNTERS

A habitual bunter could be the lead-off batter. Or you might find this type farther down in the batting order, but not normally in the three through five positions. You can expect the bunter to be a fast runner. Bunters want to dump a bunt down a foul line and beat the throw to first base. Or with a runner on third, there may be an attempted squeeze play. If the batter doesn't square around until your pitch is nearly on its way, there is very little you can do other than make the play. However, if the bunter squares early, you should react by throwing a high pitch.

Most bunters square around to face the pitcher, holding the bat level at about waist or chest level. To bunt a high pitch, they must move the bat upward to make contact. The high pitch is hard to bunt. If contact is made, the upward bat movement usually results in a foul tip or a pop-up.

WHEN BATTER HAS YOU TIMED

Batters will try to time your fastball, and that's why changing speeds is so important. On a swing and miss you can see if the bat goes through the strike zone the same time as the pitch. Another way is to watch foul balls. A batter has your fastball timed when a foul ball goes straight back toward the backstop. Change both the speed and location of your next pitch.

A right-handed batter who hits a foul outside the first-base line is swinging late. The batter hasn't caught up to your fastball; don't allow it. A right-handed batter swinging ahead of your pitch will rip a foul outside of third base. Throw a change-up and watch the batter try to hold back the swing.

DEALING WITH UMPIRES

Don't try. The umpire has a job, you have yours. Both of you should go about your business with a minimum of interaction or fuss. Umpires will blow a call at times but you must not react, no matter how bad it might seem. There is nothing you can do to change a call. Keep your cool and stick to your job. The less expression you show the umpire, the better. Umpires do not react favorably to pitchers who beg for strikes or protest calls, and they certainly don't appreciate help offered by either pitchers or catchers.

Some umpires may show a clear bias in their strike zone. You may notice that you're getting called strikes on certain pitch locations where you don't expect them. The location could be anywhere around the strike zone: low pitches, pitches off a corner, or high pitches may consistently be called strikes. When you find a strike zone bias, use it. Continue to spot pitch to the batters as you normally would, knowing that a pitch to the location where you found a bias will usually be a called strike.

OWNING THE HITTERS

Success breeds success. As you become more skilled at spotting pitches and working on the batter's timing, you will seem to "own" certain batters. The tougher you are on them, the less they will want to face you. This only adds to their tension and stress in later games. A psychological edge like this can be a powerful one in your favor. You may not be able to regularly overpower hitters, but a smart-thinking pitcher doesn't need to.

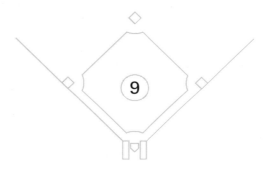

PITCHING TO WIN

THE CRITICAL SIX INCHES

The difference between a winning pitcher and a thrower is only six inches. That critical six inches is the part between your ears. Almost any player with adequate mechanics can go to the mound and fling pitches. The pitcher also throws pitches but has a reason or purpose for each pitch. The pitcher thinks of ways to control the batters. The thrower just rears back and throws. Sure, the pitchers will make some mistakes, but they will learn from them. Throwers don't learn, they just throw. This chapter is to help you learn to use that critical six inches between your ears to be a winner.

YOUR NATURAL ADVANTAGE

There is an old baseball saying that "good pitching will beat good hitting any time." Hitters will argue with this, but the averages are in favor of the pitcher. The very best hitters in your league will likely have about a .400 batting average. That means that the best hitter you'll face gets a hit four out of ten times at bat. Most team batting averages are usually around .250 or two and a half hits for each ten at bats. This computes to a team getting only six or seven hits in a six-inning game. This is part of your advantage. The odds are pretty good that you can scatter six or seven hits and win most of your games, right?

Another part of the pitcher's advantage is physical. A batter must try to hit a round ball squarely with a round bat into fair territory. This is a tough job when the hit must also be where a fielder can't make a play. The final edge is that you know what your next pitch will be and the batter does not. Having a purpose for each pitch is your best way to fool the batters.

To be a winning pitcher, you need to hold on to your advantage. Avoid giving up your advantage by walking or hitting batters or making fielding errors. Teammates who make fielding errors can also take away some of your edge. Your response must be to bear down and get the next batter.

THE OTHER TEAM'S LINEUP

Always know what part of the other team's batting order you are pitching to. Include your catcher in these conversations, if possible. Check with the scorer to see what batters did the last time you faced them. Any information on batters' tendencies from your scouting or the book can give you an edge the next time you face them. It can help both you and the catcher decide how you will work the batters.

The bottom of the order will have the weakest hitters. These are in the seven, eight, and nine positions. Normally you go after these batters with good, hard fastballs, wasting few pitches. Walking or otherwise losing one of these weaker hitters can spell trouble because the top of the order will be coming to bat. Don't relax because these are in the light end of the batting order. Bear down and you should have a couple of easy innings each time this part of the order bats.

The better hitters on the other team will be at the top of the order. The first four or five hitters in the lineup will have the best batting averages. Pitch to these batters carefully. They can bring trouble. One of the best weapons is a first-pitch strike. Many of these batters will look at one strike before getting down to business. The first-pitch strike lets the batter know you mean business and gets you started ahead in the count.

Mix your fastball and change-up on following pitches and throw strikes to stay ahead in the count. Keep pressure on all batters and make them swing at your pitch, not the one they want to take out of the lot.

IT'S YOUR GAME

When you take the ball on the mound, it's your ball game. The umpire can call "play" but nothing happens until you pitch. You have control of the game. Let your confidence show in the way you handle yourself. Send a message to the other team that you are to be dealt with. Be businesslike as you groom the mound and make your warm-up pitches. Act like you belong there and are enjoying yourself. Put on your best pokerface so the batters won't be able to read anything from your expressions.

There is an old gamblers' saying that "scared money never wins." Scared pitchers don't either. If you look worried, nervous, or timid, batters think they have you on the run. They will dig in even deeper and may hit anything you throw. Show no sign of weakness and don't hesitate. Just matter-of-factly go to work at getting them out.

You control the pace of the game. The rule that you must deliver a pitch within twenty seconds is seldom enforced. This allows you to speed up or slow the game to suit your needs. This is a tool you have learned to use against certain batters, especially nervous or anxious batters. You select your pitches. The batter can only guess where and how fast they will be.

SPOT YOUR PITCHES

The power zone for most batters is at or above the waist. Ask your catcher to hold a low target most of the time. Keep your pitches low in the strike zone and you'll have most of the batters at a disadvantage. Mostly they'll whiff at a low pitch and when they do make contact, it usually results in a harmless foul ball, pop-up, or ground ball. A pitch on the inside corner just off the kneecaps is almost unhittable. The few good low-ball hitters you'll find will be easy to remember. You can pitch differently to them with high pitches.

Mix it up a bit. When you're burning in low strikes, go high once in a while. A batter with a two-strike count who suddenly sees a pitch above the shoulders usually can't resist going after it. This is a good strike-out pitch. Batters bite at high pitches up but just below their eyes. Just make sure it is really high and not down in the power zone.

Most teams take batting practice with a pitching machine. Machines are so accurate that they can throw perfect strikes on each pitch. Batters soon learn to time and really jump on constant-speed pitches down the middle. Only the best batters learn to "go with the pitch" by hitting an outside pitch to the opposite field or pulling an inside pitch.

Another good spot pitch is right at a batter's fists. With the catcher directly behind the plate, the spot to throw at is the catcher's left shoulder for a right-handed batter. Handle-hit balls are usually easy outs. You've got to be careful not to miss and throw one down the middle because it may be hit out of the yard. There are other spots to pitch to certain batters and these were covered in Chapter 8.

MIX SPEEDS

The essence of smart pitching is the ability to mess with the batter's timing. No pitcher, even the hardest throwers in the big leagues, can blow their fastball by all the batters, and you probably can't in your league either. These batters train on a pitching machine. They've seen faster stuff than you've likely got and have learned to time pitches. Ever wonder how a pitcher can breeze through the lineup for the first three innings and start getting lit up in the fourth? The answer is simple. If the pitcher is relying on only the fastball, the batters have that pitcher timed.

The best way to keep the batters off balance and guessing is to mix in change-ups with your fastballs. The change-up you practiced throwing now becomes the perfect complement to your fastball. Throw it with the same motion as your fastball but with 15 or 20 percent less speed. The batter will usually half-swing before the ball reaches the plate. Good change-ups that are hit are usually pulled into foul territory. Once you make batters look silly, they usually start guessing. Now you have the upper hand in a head game. It should make your fastball more effective because batters don't know what to expect. Always rely on your fastball; the change-up is your upsetter pitch.

WORKING THE COUNT

We've already talked about the importance of the first-pitch strike. It gets you ahead in the count and serves notice to the batter. A second strike puts real pressure on the batter. Remember, most batters want to hit. Conventional baseball wisdom has it that on an 0 and 2 count, you should throw your next pitch out of the strike zone. This is good advice when pitching to most hitters. With two-strike pressure on them, you want to make them chase a bad pitch. However, if you have a late swinger at the plate, go with your best fastball.

You still have the edge when the count is 1 and 2. You can pitch to the better hitters more carefully and blow the ball past the weaker ones. With a 2 and 2 count, make them hit your pitch. You want this to be a pitch of decision. If you miss and the count goes full, you lose some of your advantage. With a full count, or 3 and 1, throw strikes. Remember your natural advantage, trust your defense, and make batters hit their way on base.

LEARNING TO WIN

Winning pitchers are thinkers. They learn from things that go well as well as from mistakes they make. It is a good habit to reflect on a game while it is fresh in your mind. Remember the good things that happened that you want to repeat. If you had problems, think about ways you can improve your performance the next time. Winning pitchers never stop learning. Your pitching career is just beginning. Developing that critical six inches between your ears is one of the most important things you can do to become a winning pitcher.

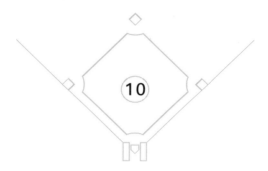

FIELDING YOUR POSITION

The instant you release the ball, you become a fielder. How well you field your position can have a big impact on the game's outcome. In a regulation six-inning Little League game, you only need to put the other team out eighteen times. There will be opportunities in each game for pitchers to help the cause with their fielding. Poor fielding that allows runners to reach base safely or advance to bases only leads to trouble. Each batter or runner that you help retire with your fielding is one less you'll have to face at the plate.

A coach should spend time during practices drilling pitchers and infielders on plays until they become almost automatic. Practicing game situations like fielding comebacks, bunts, and pop-ups with runners on base helps the infield learn to work together as a team. Knowing when and where to make the plays and being able to execute them well saves runs and makes a big contribution to winning games.

PITCHER'S FOLLOW-THROUGH

When you complete a pitch, your body should be squared, facing the plate. Keep your weight on the balls of your feet. Hold your glove at waist level and be

Pitcher's follow-through position

ready to catch any ball that is hit in your direction. In this position, you are ready to react as needed to any play. Review Chapter 3 for more on mechanics.

HARD COMEBACKERS

For some reason, good pitchers get a lot of balls hit back to them. Some balls are hit really hard, requiring you to move quickly. In any case, you must know the situation with any runners on base. Before pitching, take a couple of seconds to think about where you'll make the play if the ball is hit back to you. On a hard comeback ground ball, you have plenty of time to make a play. If there are no runners on base, field the ball, take your time, set your feet, step toward first, and make a medium-hard toss to the first-baseman.

The runners in Little League can't legally leave a base until the ball has reached the batter. A runner must run sixty feet to safely reach the next base. You should be able to force out a lead runner on any hard-hit comeback grounder. With a runner on first, the play is to second base. The shortstop will usually be covering second. Don't rush the throw. You want to be sure to get the force. The force play at second keeps the lead runner out of scoring position. It's a bonus when the infielder makes a good relay to first to complete a double play.

If there are runners on first and second, make the play to your third-baseman. Again, don't rush the throw. The third-baseman may be able to complete a double play to first but you want to be sure of forcing the lead runner. The first play is to the plate when the bases are loaded. This gets an out and saves a run, at least for the moment. Forcing the lead runner in these situations can be a big inning killer to the other team.

You don't have a force play if there is no runner on first but there are runners on either second or third. When you get a hard comeback grounder, turn and take a quick look to see if each runner is close to the base. Pick off any runner that is attempting to advance. Throw to the fielder at the advance base and let the fielder make the putout or trap the runner in a run-down. If runners are close to the base, look them back and then throw the batter out at first. Many young pitchers are so conscious of getting the sure out that they automatically go to first without looking runners back. This can either allow runners to score or advance to a scoring position.

A line drive back through the box may undress or even hit you if you don't catch it. This is why you need to be alert and in a good fielding position when you follow through. However, you should be able to catch most of the harder liners and all of the little looping liners hit toward the mound. These fly balls present an opportunity to double off any runners that have left a base when the ball was contacted.

SLOW ROLLERS

Some weak, softly hit, slow-rolling ground balls can be a difficult fielding chance for a pitcher. Because these balls are lightly hit, throwing the batter out at first may be your only play. Remember, you don't ever go far wrong when you get an out. There may be runners on base who advance on a slow-roller. Take the out at first and work out of the jam by going after the next batter.

BUNTS

Batters can bunt almost any pitch. A pitcher who has difficulty fielding bunts is headed for trouble. A team that finds the pitcher's weaknesses when they try to handle bunts can literally bunt those pitchers out of a game. Learning to field bunts well takes lots of practice. You need to learn to get to a bunt quickly and make a fast, accurate throw. Usually your only play is to first base. But if the bunt is hit hard and back toward the mound, you may force a lead runner at second or third.

A bunt that doesn't travel as far as the infield grass should be played by the catcher. The catcher should call you off as the play is made. Your coach may have a special defensive set for sacrifice bunt situations, but normally the first- and third-basemen will take bunts along the foul lines that travel more than halfway to the base. All other bunts are yours.

POP-UPS

When a batter hits the very bottom of the ball, it results in a pop-up. A short looping pop-up should be played by any fielder it is hit toward. High pop-ups must be called by the infielder making the play. The infielder must call "I've got it" loud and clear several times to avoid a collision with another fielder. Many coaches don't want a pitcher to field high pop-ups. They prefer that an infielder or the catcher handle them.

COVERING FIRST BASE

When any ground ball is hit to the right side of the infield, the pitcher must move toward first base to cover it. If the ball is fielded by the second-baseman and the first-baseman is at the bag, the pitcher pulls up and stays out of the play. The pitcher also pulls up when the first-baseman waves the pitcher off, which signals that the first-baseman will cover the bag or make the play unassisted.

The pitcher will cover first when the first-baseman cannot make the play. The pitcher should run toward a point on the foul line ten to fifteen feet short of first base, then turn and run along and inside of the foul line toward first to avoid a collision with the runner. After reaching the bag, the pitcher should take the throw and step on the infield side of the bag.

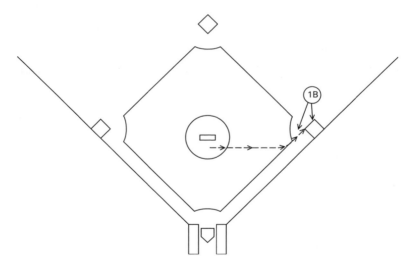

COVERING FIRST BASE
The pitcher goes toward the first-base line (dotted line) then turns and runs along the line in fair territory toward first base. Staying inside the line should help avoid any contact with the runner. The infielder should toss the ball to the pitcher as he nears first base.

The pitcher must hustle to cover first. There isn't a lot of time for the pitcher to get to the base ahead of the runner. Most of the plays are relatively close, even when everything is done properly. A pitcher who loafs or hesitates will not get the job done.

COVERING OTHER BASES

Pitchers must also back up plays at third base and home plate. They must anticipate where the play will be and go quickly to a backup position in foul territory behind the fielder covering the base. If it is not certain where the play will be, the pitcher should go to a point between third and home and then move as the play develops. The proper position when backing up a base is far enough behind the fielder to catch any missed ball or overthrow.

The pitcher covers home plate when a pitch gets by the catcher and there is a runner on third base. The pitcher must break toward the plate the instant the pitch gets by the catcher. The runner must go sixty feet to score. The pitcher needs to move about forty feet to reach the plate. A hustling pitcher should always win this race and be in a position to put the runner out.

As pitchers reach the plate, they should stop in fair territory, about two feet up the line toward third. This is the position to take the throw from the catcher and tag the approaching runner. A pitcher should never attempt to block the plate because collisions at the plate can result in serious injuries. If possible, pitchers should try to make a swipe tag on the runner while keeping their legs and body clear of the runner's path.

YOUR FIELDING ADVANTAGE

Because you play other defensive positions regularly when you aren't pitching, you should be able to make plays on all comeback hits. Your main concentration should be on where to make the plays and getting to your coverage assignments. Lack of hustle in carrying out your assignments can be costly. Help yourself with good alert fielding. It's a big part of becoming a winning pitcher.

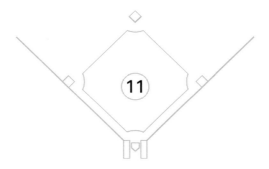

FINAL THOUGHTS

As the pitcher you are the key defensive player on the field. How well you perform personally will have a big bearing on any game's outcome. There is pressure on a pitcher. Good pitchers relish it. You may even look forward to it. But you don't need to feel that all of the weight of the game is on your shoulders. After all, baseball is a team sport. You have eight teammates on the field to provide defensive support and score runs.

Don't expect to win every game. Regardless of how bad you may want a perfect record, it's an expectation you probably can't meet. Baseball is a funny game; a game of inches. There are many variables in the course of a baseball game that can determine the outcome.

Breaks go both ways. The best team doesn't always win. The best pitcher doesn't always win. Sometimes you will pitch well but your fielders will boot the ball all over the park. The other team's pitcher may shut down your batters and they don't score enough runs to win. Other times you won't have your best stuff, but each ball the other team hits results in an easy out. You have to condition yourself to learn from game situations and keep your confidence. Don't lose your confidence and never stop learning. You have a lot of baseball ahead of you in the years to come.

From all of our years of coaching, our best advice is this: Go to the mound mentally and physically prepared to give it your very best, and be willing to accept the outcome. No one can expect any more of you. Leave the mound at the end of the game with your head high, knowing you gave it your best. And, above all, have fun.

ABOUT THE AUTHORS

Don Oster has been coaching youth baseball at the highest level for decades. In 1985, as manager of a team from East Tonka, Minnesota, he went to the Little League World Series. From 1987 to 1991, his Babe Ruth League team, for which he was the pitching coach, appeared in four consecutive World Series. He is also the author of *Largemouth Bass* and is the coauthor of *Hunting Today's Whitetail.* He lives in southern Indiana.

Bill McMillan has twenty years' experience coaching youth baseball as a manager and a pitching coach. His teams have won nine league championships and a Minnesota State Little League championship. He has served as a pitching coach for youth aged nine to sixteen. He has been a public school teacher and a university professor. He holds a Ph.D. in educational psychology and has worked extensively at the state and national levels on various educational programs.